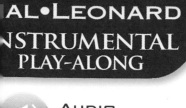

HAL•LEONARD
INSTRUMENTAL
PLAY-ALONG

AUDIO
ACCESS
INCLUDED

PLAYBACK+
Speed • Pitch • Balance • Loop

TRUMPET

GREAT CLASSICAL THEMES

Audio Arrangements by Peter Deneff

To access audio visit:
www.halleonard.com/mylibrary

Enter Code
5446-4611-7905-1734

ISBN 978-1-5400-5039-7

HAL•LEONARD®

Visit Hal Leonard Online at
www.halleonard.com

Contact us:
Hal Leonard
7777 West Bluemound Road
Milwaukee, WI 53213
Email: info@halleonard.com

In Europe, contact:
Hal Leonard Europe Limited
42 Wigmore Street
Marylebone, London, W1U 2RN
Email: info@halleonardeurope.com

In Australia, contact:
Hal Leonard Australia Pty. Ltd.
4 Lentara Court
Cheltenham, Victoria, 3192 Australia
Email: info@halleonard.com.au

CONTENTS

BLUE DANUBE WALTZ
Op. 314

TRUMPET

By JOHANN STRAUSS, JR.

CAN CAN
from ORPHEUS IN THE UNDERWORLD

TRUMPET

By JACQUES OFFENBACH

EINE KLEINE NACHTMUSIK

("Serenade")

(First Movement Theme)

TRUMPET

By WOLFGANG AMADEUS MOZART

GRAND MARCH
from AÏDA

By GIUSEPPE VERDI

TRUMPET

HABANERA
from CARMEN

TRUMPET

By GEORGES BIZET

HORNPIPE
from WATER MUSIC

TRUMPET

By GEORGE FRIDERIC HANDEL

Allegro maestoso

HUNGARIAN DANCE NO. 5

TRUMPET

By JOHANNES BRAHMS

JESU, JOY OF MAN'S DESIRING

from CANTATA 147
BWV 147

By JOHANN SEBASTIAN BACH

TRUMPET

LARGO

from SYMPHONY NO. 9 IN E MINOR
"FROM THE NEW WORLD"

TRUMPET

By ANTONÍN DVOŘÁK

MORNING MOOD
from PEER GYNT

TRUMPET

By EDVARD GRIEG

ODE TO JOY
from SYMPHONY NO. 9 IN D MINOR

TRUMPET

By LUDWIG VAN BEETHOVEN

THE SORCERER'S APPRENTICE

TRUMPET

By PAUL DUKAS

SPRING
from THE FOUR SEASONS

TRUMPET

By ANTONIO VIVALDI

THE SURPRISE SYMPHONY
from SYMPHONY NO. 94, SECOND MOVEMENT THEME

TRUMPET

By FRANZ JOSEPH HAYDN

WILLIAM TELL OVERTURE
Theme

TRUMPET

By GIOACHINO ROSSINI

HAL•LEONARD INSTRUMENTAL PLAY-ALONG

Your favorite songs are arranged just for solo instrumentalists with this outstanding series. Each book includes great full-accompaniment play-along audio so you can sound just like a pro! Check out **www.halleonard.com** to see all the titles available.

The Beatles

All You Need Is Love • Blackbird • Day Tripper • Eleanor Rigby • Get Back • Here, There and Everywhere • Hey Jude • I Will • Let It Be • Lucy in the Sky with Diamonds • Ob-La-Di, Ob-La-Da • Penny Lane • Something • Ticket to Ride • Yesterday.

00225330	Flute	$14.99
00225331	Clarinet	$14.99
00225332	Alto Sax	$14.99
00225333	Tenor Sax	$14.99
00225334	Trumpet	$14.99
00225335	Horn	$14.99
00225336	Trombone	$14.99
00225337	Violin	$14.99
00225338	Viola	$14.99
00225339	Cello	$14.99

Chart Hits

All About That Bass • All of Me • Happy • Radioactive • Roar • Say Something • Shake It Off • A Sky Full of Stars • Someone like You • Stay with Me • Thinking Out Loud • Uptown Funk.

00146207	Flute	$12.99
00146208	Clarinet	$12.99
00146209	Alto Sax	$12.99
00146210	Tenor Sax	$12.99
00146211	Trumpet	$12.99
00146212	Horn	$12.99
00146213	Trombone	$12.99
00146214	Violin	$12.99
00146215	Viola	$12.99
00146216	Cello	$12.99

Disney Greats

Arabian Nights • Hawaiian Roller Coaster Ride • It's a Small World • Look Through My Eyes • Yo Ho (A Pirate's Life for Me) • and more.

00841934	Flute	$12.99
00841935	Clarinet	$12.99
00841936	Alto Sax	$12.99
00841937	Tenor Sax	$12.95
00841938	Trumpet	$12.99
00841939	Horn	$12.99
00841940	Trombone	$12.99
00841941	Violin	$12.99
00841942	Viola	$12.99
00841943	Cello	$12.99
00842078	Oboe	$12.99

The Greatest Showman

Come Alive • From Now On • The Greatest Show • A Million Dreams • Never Enough • The Other Side • Rewrite the Stars • This Is Me • Tightrope.

00277389	Flute	$14.99
00277390	Clarinet	$14.99
00277391	Alto Sax	$14.99
00277392	Tenor Sax	$14.99
00277393	Trumpet	$14.99
00277394	Horn	$14.99
00277395	Trombone	$14.99
00277396	Violin	$14.99
00277397	Viola	$14.99
00277398	Cello	$14.99

Movie and TV Music

The Avengers • Doctor Who XI • Downton Abbey • Game of Thrones • Guardians of the Galaxy • Hawaii Five-O • Married Life • Rey's Theme (from *Star Wars: The Force Awakens*) • The X-Files • and more.

00261807	Flute	$12.99
00261808	Clarinet	$12.99
00261809	Alto Sax	$12.99
00261810	Tenor Sax	$12.99
00261811	Trumpet	$12.99
00261812	Horn	$12.99
00261813	Trombone	$12.99
00261814	Violin	$12.99
00261815	Viola	$12.99
00261816	Cello	$12.99

12 Pop Hits

Believer • Can't Stop the Feeling • Despacito • It Ain't Me • Look What You Made Me Do • Million Reasons • Perfect • Send My Love (To Your New Lover) • Shape of You • Slow Hands • Too Good at Goodbyes • What About Us.

00261790	Flute	$12.99
00261791	Clarinet	$12.99
00261792	Alto Sax	$12.99
00261793	Tenor Sax	$12.99
00261794	Trumpet	$12.99
00261795	Horn	$12.99
00261796	Trombone	$12.99
00261797	Violin	$12.99
00261798	Viola	$12.99
00261799	Cello	$12.99

Songs from Frozen, Tangled and Enchanted

Do You Want to Build a Snowman? • For the First Time in Forever • Happy Working Song • I See the Light • In Summer • Let It Go • Mother Knows Best • That's How You Know • True Love's First Kiss • When Will My Life Begin • and more.

00126921	Flute	$14.99
00126922	Clarinet	$14.99
00126923	Alto Sax	$14.99
00126924	Tenor Sax	$14.99
00126925	Trumpet	$14.99
00126926	Horn	$14.99
00126927	Trombone	$14.99
00126928	Violin	$14.99
00126929	Viola	$14.99
00126930	Cello	$14.99

Top Hits

Adventure of a Lifetime • Budapest • Die a Happy Man • Ex's & Oh's • Fight Song • Hello • Let It Go • Love Yourself • One Call Away • Pillowtalk • Stitches • Writing's on the Wall.

00171073	Flute	$12.99
00171074	Clarinet	$12.99
00171075	Alto Sax	$12.99
00171106	Tenor Sax	$12.99
00171107	Trumpet	$12.99
00171108	Horn	$12.99
00171109	Trombone	$12.99
00171110	Violin	$12.99
00171111	Viola	$12.99
00171112	Cello	$12.99

Wicked

As Long As You're Mine • Dancing Through Life • Defying Gravity • For Good • I'm Not That Girl • Popular • The Wizard and I • and more.

00842236	Flute	$12.99
00842237	Clarinet	$12.99
00842238	Alto Saxophone	$12.99
00842239	Tenor Saxophone	$11.95
00842240	Trumpet	$12.99
00842241	Horn	$12.99
00842242	Trombone	$12.99
00842243	Violin	$12.99
00842244	Viola	$12.99
00842245	Cello	$12.99

HAL•LEONARD®

101 SONGS

BIG COLLECTIONS OF FAVORITE SONGS ARRANGED FOR SOLO INSTRUMENTALISTS.

101 BROADWAY SONGS

00154199	Flute	$14.99
00154200	Clarinet	$14.99
00154201	Alto Sax	$14.99
00154202	Tenor Sax	$14.99
00154203	Trumpet	$14.99
00154204	Horn	$14.99
00154205	Trombone	$14.99
00154206	Violin	$14.99
00154207	Viola	$14.99
00154208	Cello	$14.99

101 HIT SONGS

00194561	Flute	$16.99
00197182	Clarinet	$16.99
00197183	Alto Sax	$16.99
00197184	Tenor Sax	$16.99
00197185	Trumpet	$16.99
00197186	Horn	$16.99
00197187	Trombone	$16.99
00197188	Violin	$16.99
00197189	Viola	$16.99
00197190	Cello	$16.99

101 CHRISTMAS SONGS

00278637	Flute	$14.99
00278638	Clarinet	$14.99
00278639	Alto Sax	$14.99
00278640	Tenor Sax	$14.99
00278641	Trumpet	$14.99
00278642	Horn	$14.99
00278643	Trombone	$14.99
00278644	Violin	$14.99
00278645	Viola	$14.99
00278646	Cello	$14.99

101 JAZZ SONGS

00146363	Flute	$14.99
00146364	Clarinet	$14.99
00146366	Alto Sax	$14.99
00146367	Tenor Sax	$14.99
00146368	Trumpet	$14.99
00146369	Horn	$14.99
00146370	Trombone	$14.99
00146371	Violin	$14.99
00146372	Viola	$14.99
00146373	Cello	$14.99

101 CLASSICAL THEMES

00155315	Flute	$14.99
00155317	Clarinet	$14.99
00155318	Alto Sax	$14.99
00155319	Tenor Sax	$14.99
00155320	Trumpet	$14.99
00155321	Horn	$14.99
00155322	Trombone	$14.99
00155323	Violin	$14.99
00155324	Viola	$14.99
00155325	Cello	$14.99

101 MOVIE HITS

00158087	Flute	$14.99
00158088	Clarinet	$14.99
00158089	Alto Sax	$14.99
00158090	Tenor Sax	$14.99
00158091	Trumpet	$14.99
00158092	Horn	$14.99
00158093	Trombone	$14.99
00158094	Violin	$14.99
00158095	Viola	$14.99
00158096	Cello	$14.99

101 DISNEY SONGS

00244104	Flute	$16.99
00244106	Clarinet	$16.99
00244107	Alto Sax	$16.99
00244108	Tenor Sax	$16.99
00244109	Trumpet	$16.99
00244112	Horn	$16.99
00244120	Trombone	$16.99
00244121	Violin	$16.99
00244125	Viola	$16.99
00244126	Cello	$16.99

101 POPULAR SONGS

00224722	Flute	$16.99
00224723	Clarinet	$16.99
00224724	Alto Sax	$16.99
00224725	Tenor Sax	$16.99
00224726	Trumpet	$16.99
00224727	Horn	$16.99
00224728	Trombone	$16.99
00224729	Violin	$16.99
00224730	Viola	$16.99
00224731	Cello	$16.99

HAL•LEONARD®
www.halleonard.com

Prices, contents and availability subject to change without notice.

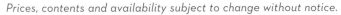

101 TIPS FROM HAL LEONARD

STUFF ALL THE PROS KNOW AND USE

Ready to take your skills to the next level? These books present valuable how-to insight that musicians of all styles and levels can benefit from. The text, photos, music, diagrams and accompanying audio provide a terrific, easy-to-use resource for a variety of topics.

101 HAMMOND B-3 TIPS
by Brian Charette
Topics include: funky scales and modes; unconventional harmonies; creative chord voicings; cool drawbar settings; ear-grabbing special effects; professional gigging advice; practicing effectively; making good use of the pedals; and much more!
00128918 Book/Online Audio $14.99

101 HARMONICA TIPS
by Steve Cohen
Topics include: techniques, position playing, soloing, accompaniment, the blues, equipment, performance, maintenance, and much more!
00821040 Book/Online Audio $16.99

101 CELLO TIPS—2ND EDITION
by Angela Schmidt
Topics include: bowing techniques, non-classical playing, electric cellos, accessories, gig tips, practicing, recording and much more!
00149094 Book/Online Audio $14.99

101 FLUTE TIPS
by Elaine Schmidt
Topics include: selecting the right flute for you, finding the right teacher, warm-up exercises, practicing effectively, taking good care of your flute, gigging advice, staying and playing healthy, and much more.
00119883 Book/CD Pack..................................$14.99

101 SAXOPHONE TIPS
by Eric Morones
Topics include: techniques; maintenance; equipment; practicing; recording; performance; and much more!
00311082 Book/CD Pack..................................$15.99

101 TRUMPET TIPS
by Scott Barnard
Topics include: techniques, articulation, tone production, soloing, exercises, special effects, equipment, performance, maintenance and much more.
00312082 Book/CD Pack..................................$14.99

101 UPRIGHT BASS TIPS
by Andy McKee
Topics include: right- and left-hand technique, improvising and soloing, practicing, proper care of the instrument, ear training, performance, and much more.
00102009 Book/Online Audio $14.99

101 BASS TIPS
by Gary Willis
Topics include: techniques, improvising and soloing, equipment, practicing, ear training, performance, theory, and much more.
00695542 Book/Online Audio $17.99

101 DRUM TIPS—2ND EDITION
Topics include: grooves, practicing, warming up, tuning, gear, performance, and much more!
00151936 Book/Online Audio $14.99

101 FIVE-STRING BANJO TIPS
by Fred Sokolow
Topics include: techniques, ear training, performance, and much more!
00696647 Book/CD Pack..................................$14.99

101 GUITAR TIPS
by Adam St. James
Topics include: scales, music theory, truss rod adjustments, proper recording studio set-ups, and much more. The book also features snippets of advice from some of the most celebrated guitarists and producers in the music business.
00695737 Book/Online Audio $16.99

101 MANDOLIN TIPS
by Fred Sokolow
Topics include: playing tips, practicing tips, accessories, mandolin history and lore, practical music theory, and much more!
00119493 Book/Online Audio $14.99

101 RECORDING TIPS
by Adam St. James
This book contains recording tips, suggestions, and advice learned firsthand from legendary producers, engineers, and artists. These tricks of the trade will improve anyone's home or pro studio recordings.
00311035 Book/CD Pack..................................$14.95

101 UKULELE TIPS
by Fred Sokolow with Ronny Schiff
Topics include: techniques, improvising and soloing, equipment, practicing, ear training, performance, uke history and lore, and much more!
00696596 Book/Online Audio $15.99

101 VIOLIN TIPS
by Angela Schmidt
Topics include: bowing techniques, non-classical playing, electric violins, accessories, gig tips, practicing, recording, and much more!
00842672 Book/CD Pack..................................$14.99

Prices, contents and availability subject to change without notice.

HAL•LEONARD®
www.halleonard.com